# MILK & DAIRY PRODUCTS

HEALTHY EATING

BY GEMMA McMULLEN

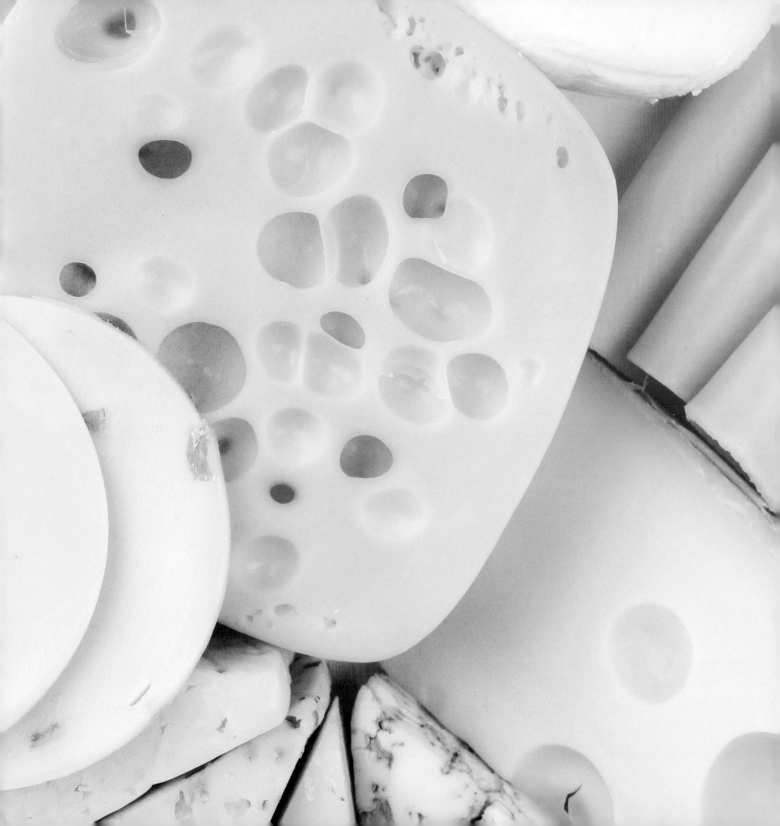

# CONTENTS

Words that look like this can be found in the glossary on page 24.

**BookLife**
PUBLISHING

©2022
BookLife Publishing Ltd.
King's Lynn, Norfolk
PE30 4LS, UK

ISBN: 978-1-83927-443-5

**Written by:**
Gemma McMullen

**Edited by:**
Harriet Brundle

**Designed by:**
Ian McMullen
& Drue Rintoul

A catalogue record for this book is available from the British Library.

# WHAT ARE MILK AND DAIRY PRODUCTS?

Milk is a white liquid made in the bodies of some animals. Milk can be drunk or made into food. Most of the milk that we use comes from cows.

Foods that are made from milk are called dairy products. They include cheese and yoghurt.

# MILK

Having milk in your diet is important because it helps to keep your teeth and bones strong.

Milk can be used as a drink. It is often put with cereal.

Adults put milk in hot drinks such as tea.

# WHERE DOES MILK COME FROM?

Most milk comes from cows. Farmers keep dairy cows just for their milk. On large farms, special machines take the milk from the cows.

The milk is prepared by special machines before it is put into bottles.

Milk needs to be kept cold in the fridge.

# CHEESE

Cheese is a food that is made using milk. It is usually made in special factories and can take quite a long time to make.

There are lots of different types of cheese, each with different flavours.

Cheese has a longer shelf life than milk.

# YOGHURT

Yoghurt is a product made using milk. Natural yoghurt is sour in taste, so yoghurt is often made sweeter before it is sold.

Yoghurt can be made sweeter using fruit or honey, but sweetened yoghurt often contains a lot of sugar.

# BUTTER

Butter is a dairy product. Milk is churned to separate the fat from the milk. Butter is made using the fat.

Butter is often spread on toast or used as an ingredient in baking.

# HEALTHY DAIRY PRODUCTS

Milk and dairy products are good for our bodies because they contain important proteins and minerals.

Some dairy products contain a lot of fat and sugar. Eating lots of these products is bad for your health.

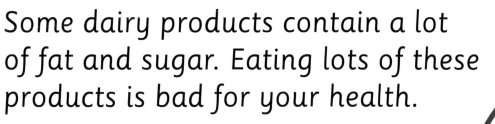

Ice cream often has a lot of fat in it.

# OTHER MILK SOURCES

Lots of animals make
milk to feed their babies.
Most dairy products are
made using cows' milk,
but milk from other
animals can also
be used.

People also drink goats' milk and sheep's milk.

# MILK FROM OTHER ANIMALS

Water buffalo are the main source of milk in South Asia.

Camels' milk contains ten times more iron than cows' milk.

Yaks' milk is high in fat, making it good for yoghurt, butter and cheese.

Reindeer milk is sometimes used in northern parts of the world.

21

# CHEESE FROM AROUND THE WORLD

Mozzarella is a cheese from Italy. It feels soft and bouncy when you touch it.

Mascarpone also comes from Italy. It is often used to make sweet foods, such as cheesecake.

Cheddar is an English cheese. It is pale yellow and hard.

Roquefort is a French cheese. In France, it is called 'the cheese of kings'.

# GLOSSARY

**churned**
mixed around to make butter

**factories**
buildings where things are made

**minerals**
important things that plants, animals and humans need to grow

**proteins**
important things that humans need to grow and repair

**shelf life**
how long a food item stays fresh

# INDEX

## PHOTO CREDITS

Photo credits: Abbreviations: l–left, r–right, b–bottom, t–top, c–centre, m–middle. All images are courtesy of Shutterstock.com. With thanks to Getty Images, Thinkstock Photo and iStockphoto. Front Cover – Anna Sedneva . 1– vipman. 2, 11 – Africa Studio. 3 – Lukas Gojda. 4 – PRUSSIA ART. 5 – Africa Studio. 5inset – Sea Wave. 6l – Jacek Chabraszewski. 6r – Patrick Foto. 7 – stockcreations. 7inset – martiapunts. 8 – Toa55. 9 – Freer. 9inset – Peter Zvonar. 10 – Wei Ming. 12 – Sunny Forest. 13 – paulaphoto. 14 – Tobik. 15 – Kitch Bain. 15inset – MAii Thitikorn.16 – Ridkous Mykhailo. 17 – M. Unal Ozmen. 17inset – Lik Studio. 18 – Eric Isselee. 19 – Dmitry Kalinovsky. 19inset – LiAndStudio. 20t – Matthew Gamble. 20b – Yasser El Dershaby. 21 – Incredible Arctic. 21inset – eAlisa. 22t – Maya Morenko. 22insetl – Ivlianna. 22insetm – Lesya Dolyuk. 22insetr – koss13. 22b – Madlen. 23t – Julia Ivantsova. 23inset – Dan Kosmayer. 23b – picturepartners.